NIGHTMARE PLAGUES

SMALLPOX
Is It Over?

by Adam Reingold

Consultant: Dr. Marc Strassburg
Adjunct Professor
Department of Epidemiology, UCLA;
Professor, Health Sciences
TUI University

BEARPORT
PUBLISHING

New York, New York

Terrible Suffering

Ali Maow Maalin (AH-lee MOU MAH-lin) started to feel sick on October 22, 1977. At first, the 23-year-old hospital cook had a burning **fever**. A few days later, a red **rash** appeared on his arms and stomach. Then the rash turned into small, painful pimple-like sores called **pustules**. On October 30, a nurse went to see the sick young man. He knew right away what had struck Maalin—the deadly disease **smallpox**!

Ali Maow Maalin

Maalin went to the hospital when he first got sick. Doctors who saw his rash mistakenly thought he had chicken pox and sent him home.

Smallpox can spread easily from one person to another. As a result, nearby health workers immediately **quarantined** Maalin. They didn't want anyone else in Merca (MER-kuh), the city in Somalia where Maalin lived, to catch the illness. After all, there is no medicine to cure smallpox once a person has the disease.

Fortunately, Maalin soon began to feel better on his own. Over the next few weeks, he completely recovered. The young man was lucky to be alive.

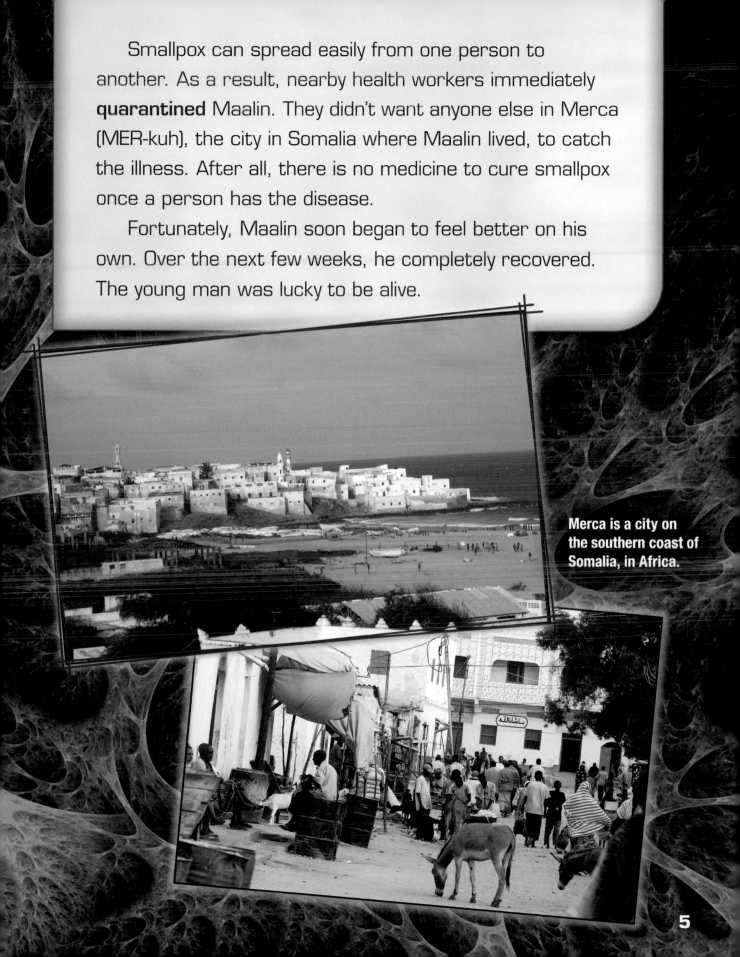

Merca is a city on the southern coast of Somalia, in Africa.

Trying to Stop a Killer

In 1967, ten years before Maalin caught smallpox, the **World Health Organization** (WHO) had started a program to get rid of the disease. Health workers were sent to Africa, Asia, and South America. Smallpox was still a threat in parts of these continents. To prevent people from getting and spreading the disease, the health workers **vaccinated** millions of people. They also looked for people who already had smallpox and vaccinated anyone who lived with them or came into contact with them.

The smallpox vaccine is given using a special needle that is dipped into a liquid vaccine. The needle is then pushed 15 times into the skin of a person's upper arm.

Health workers vaccinated this child in Ethiopia as part of their plan to get rid of smallpox.

In the hundred years before the WHO vaccination program, it is **estimated** that up to 500 million people were killed by smallpox.

The last stop to get rid of smallpox was Somalia. Following a report of an **outbreak**, a team of health workers searched the country for smallpox victims. They quarantined the ones they found. The patients were kept in huts far from other people so they couldn't spread the illness. Next, workers vaccinated anyone who might have come into contact with these sick people.

By 1977, it seemed the battle against one of the world's greatest killers was over. No more smallpox cases were reported—until Maalin. Would he be the world's last smallpox victim?

Ali Maow Maalin was the last known person to catch smallpox. He got the disease in Merca, Somalia, when he offered to help move two sick children to a quarantine camp.

Battle Inside the Body

The WHO had struggled to wipe out smallpox because the disease can be very deadly. About 30 percent of the people who catch it die. A tiny germ called a **virus** causes the disease. When a sick person coughs, sneezes, or breathes out, the virus goes into the air and can be breathed in by anyone nearby.

Although it is less common, the disease can also spread if healthy people touch the skin of a smallpox victim. The virus can get on their hands, which they may then breathe in if they touch their nose or mouth.

Once inside a person, the smallpox virus **invades** the **cells** that make up the body. The virus then makes thousands of copies of itself. It destroys the cells by breaking out of them.

Normally, the body makes a kind of **protein** called an antibody, which grabs on to viruses and stops them from moving through the body. If a person's antibodies are not strong enough, however, the viruses can damage cells that make up important **organs**, like the liver. Once these cells are damaged, the organs cannot work properly and the person may die.

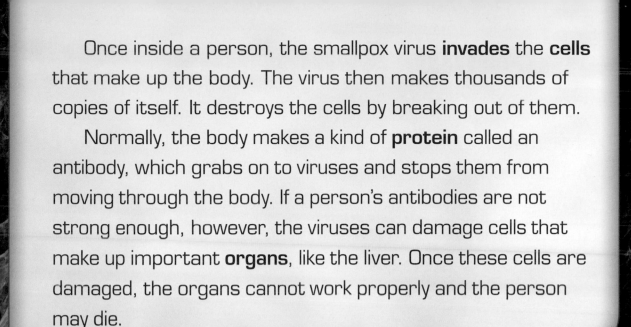

This is a close-up image of a smallpox virus. It is so tiny that the virus can be seen only with a very powerful microscope.

People who catch smallpox and survive can never get the disease again. The antibodies that their bodies made during their illness will easily fight off the virus if it appears again.

Smallpox Symptoms

How do people feel when they first become **infected** by the smallpox virus? For about the first two weeks, they don't have any **symptoms**. Then they will get a high fever—up to 104°F (40°C). They'll also have terrible headaches and achy muscles. Most victims feel too weak to do anything but rest.

Unlike many other diseases, smallpox cannot be spread by animals. Only humans can get the disease. To survive, smallpox germs need a steady supply of new human victims.

After a few days, a red rash appears all over the body—on the arms, legs, stomach, face, and even inside the mouth. In a few more days, the rash will turn into raised, painful pustules that are filled with fluid. If the patient doesn't die, the pustules will dry up, become scabs, and fall off about three weeks later. Even if a smallpox patient recovers, however, the nightmare may not be over. Smallpox causes blindness in some of its victims.

1

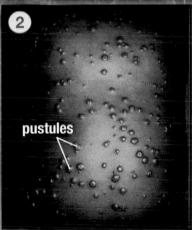

2

pustules

These photos show how smallpox pustules form on the body and then dry up and become scabs. People with smallpox can spread the disease to others until their pustules turn into scabs and fall off.

Smallpox pustules begin to appear

3 days later

3

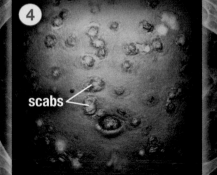

4

scabs

Most smallpox survivors are left with pitted scars where the pustules once were, especially on the face. They have to live with these scars for the rest of their lives.

4–5 days later

8–9 days later

Spreading Around the World

For thousands of years, smallpox has caused great suffering to people living in Asia, Africa, and Europe. However, the illness didn't spread to North and South America until the early 1500s. At that time, there were two great Native American empires. The Aztec controlled present-day Mexico. The Inca ruled western South America.

In 1520, Spanish **conquerors** sailed to Mexico to take over Native American lands. An African slave in the group was sick with smallpox. He triggered one of the deadliest outbreaks of all time.

Scientists who studied the mummy of Pharaoh Ramses V of Egypt believe he died from smallpox more than 3,000 years ago.

During the journey to Mexico, the African slave infected one of the Spanish soldiers on the ship. Soon after landing, the infected soldier came into contact with the Aztec—and they started getting sick. The disease slowly spread from one Native American to the next. Sufferers cried out in pain with every move. Some of them were covered with so many pustules that their loved ones could barely recognize them. The Aztec had no idea what was causing this terrible **plague**.

About 200,000 people lived in Tenochtitlán (*tay*-nohch-TEET-lahn), the capital city of the Aztec empire. Because they lived close together in cities, the Aztec easily spread the smallpox virus to one another.

Mightier Than Any Army

Smallpox nearly wiped out the Aztec. In some areas, up to 80 percent of the people were killed. The Aztec had never experienced smallpox before. They couldn't understand why they were getting sick.

Even more confusing was why the Spanish weren't dying. The Aztec didn't know that the Spanish were **immune** to the disease. Most of them had already had smallpox in Europe. Now their antibodies prevented them from getting ill. With few Native Americans healthy enough to fight, the Spanish easily defeated the Aztec.

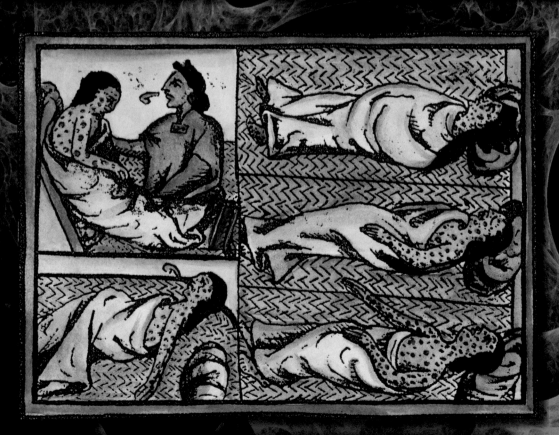

This drawing shows the Aztec suffering from smallpox. During the outbreak, so many people became sick that there was often nobody left to take care of the ill. Many died of starvation.

The disease spread rapidly among other Native American tribes. By the mid-1520s, the Spanish moved south to attack the Inca. With the help of smallpox, the Spanish conquered their empire, too. The epidemic of the 1520s killed several million Inca and Aztec. It was deadlier than any European army.

The Aztec and Inca Empires

NORTH AMERICA

Atlantic Ocean

Mexico

Pacific Ocean

SOUTH AMERICA

N
W — E
S

☐ Aztec empire
■ Inca empire

This map shows the places where the Aztec and Inca lived—and were killed by smallpox.

The Inca empire included 25,000 miles (40,234 km) of roads. Native Americans traveled quickly from place to place on these roads—and carried smallpox with them.

In 1492, the population of North and South America was about 72 million people. Within 300 years, there were only about 600,000 Native Americans left. Most had died from warfare and diseases such as smallpox.

George Washington Fights Smallpox

About 250 years after smallpox killed millions in Mexico and South America, a huge outbreak hit the British colonies in America. At the time, American soldiers were fighting in the American Revolution (1775–1783). As a result, General George Washington's troops had to battle smallpox—as well as the British army.

George Washington came down with smallpox during a trip to the Caribbean island of Barbados when he was 19 years old. The disease left him with very faint scars on his face.

To make matters worse, many British soldiers weren't getting sick from the disease. Smallpox was still more common in Europe than it was in North America. Many of the British had caught smallpox in Europe when they were younger. As a result, those who survived the disease were now immune, just like the Spanish were years before. This time, however, smallpox didn't help the Europeans enough. The Americans won the war. Still, thousands more American soldiers died of smallpox than of battle wounds.

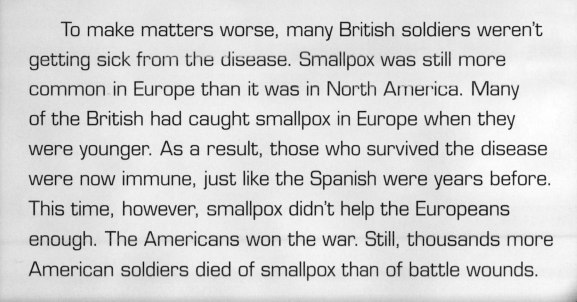

The American Revolution provided ideal conditions for the spread of smallpox. Washington's soldiers traveled long distances and slept in close quarters. The disease easily spread as the soldiers breathed and sneezed on one another.

Many American soldiers came down with smallpox right after they joined the army. As a result, thousands of men refused to sign up to fight because they were afraid of catching the disease.

Arm-to-Arm Aid

Around the same time that American soldiers were battling smallpox, doctors in Europe and America started using **variolation** to prevent the illness. This method had already been used in Asia and Africa. First, a doctor made a small cut on the arm of a healthy person. Next, **pus** was taken from inside the pustule of a smallpox victim. The pus was then put on the wound of the healthy person.

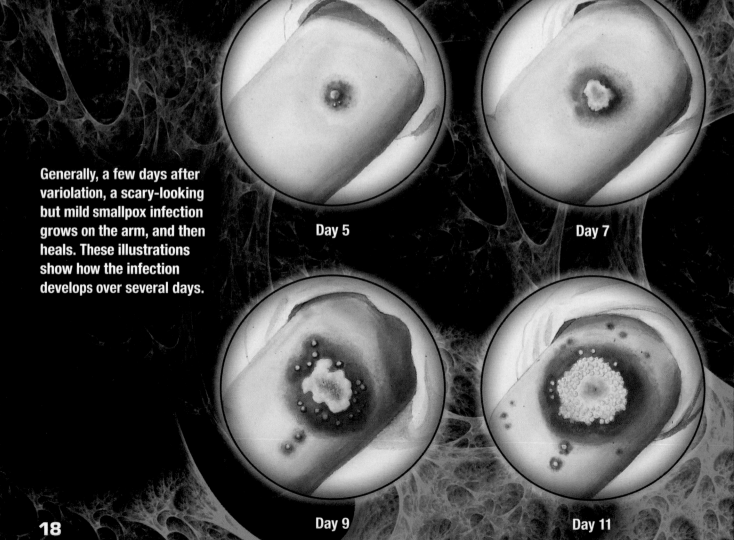

Generally, a few days after variolation, a scary-looking but mild smallpox infection grows on the arm, and then heals. These illustrations show how the infection develops over several days.

Day 5

Day 7

Day 9

Day 11

Sometimes variolation caused the person to develop a weak form of the illness. Yet it also caused the person to develop antibodies against the virus. The antibodies protected the person from getting smallpox in the future.

There were some problems with variolation, however. Some people who received it developed a serious, full-blown case of smallpox—and risked scars or blindness. About 2 percent of the people who got variolated died from this **infection**. Some people didn't want to take the risk.

This illustration from the early 1800s shows an old man with pustules on his face. Hundreds of years ago, people used to call pustules "speckles." That is how smallpox got the nickname "the speckled monster."

About 1,000 years ago in China, people were variolated in a different way—by having ground-up smallpox scabs blown into their noses. This form of variolation saved many lives, just as the arm wound method did.

Help from Cows

In 1796, Dr. Edward Jenner discovered a much safer way to protect people from smallpox than variolation. Jenner had heard stories about milkmaids who had caught a nondeadly disease from cows called cowpox. These women never got smallpox. How could this be?

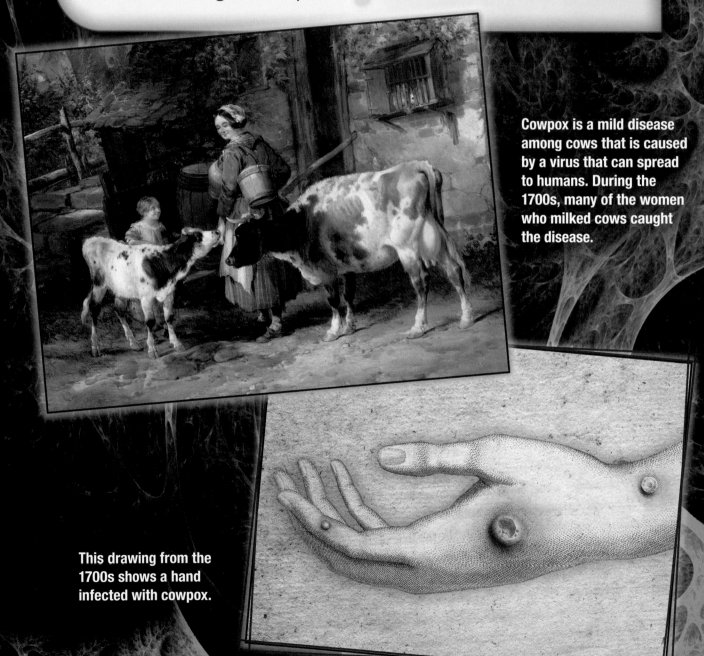

Cowpox is a mild disease among cows that is caused by a virus that can spread to humans. During the 1700s, many of the women who milked cows caught the disease.

This drawing from the 1700s shows a hand infected with cowpox.

Jenner tested a **theory**. A local milkmaid, Sarah Nelmes, had caught cowpox from a cow named Blossom. On May 4, 1796, Jenner took pus from one of Nelmes's cowpox pustules. He then put it into a small wound on the arm of a boy named James Phipps. A few weeks later, Jenner **exposed** the boy to smallpox. Nothing happened. Phipps did not get sick. Jenner had just created the first smallpox vaccine. It was a safe way to prevent infection from the deadly disease.

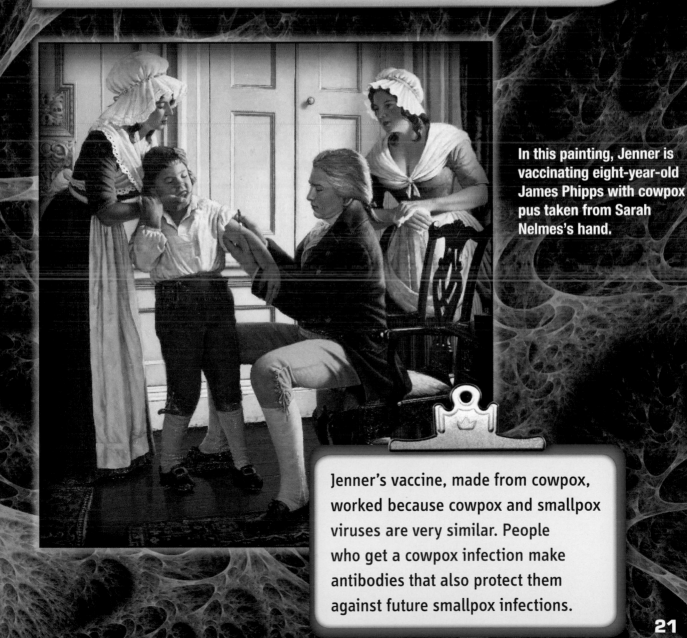

In this painting, Jenner is vaccinating eight-year-old James Phipps with cowpox pus taken from Sarah Nelmes's hand.

Jenner's vaccine, made from cowpox, worked because cowpox and smallpox viruses are very similar. People who get a cowpox infection make antibodies that also protect them against future smallpox infections.

Last Stand in New York

After Jenner's discovery, doctors began vaccinating people to prevent them from getting smallpox. Countless lives were saved. Still, smallpox continued to attack millions because vaccines weren't available to everyone.

In 1947, smallpox brought panic to New York City. A businessman from Mexico arrived by bus with the disease on March 1. He went to a local hospital on March 5 and died five days later. Unfortunately, he had already come into contact with many New Yorkers.

A vaccine provides almost complete protection from smallpox infection.

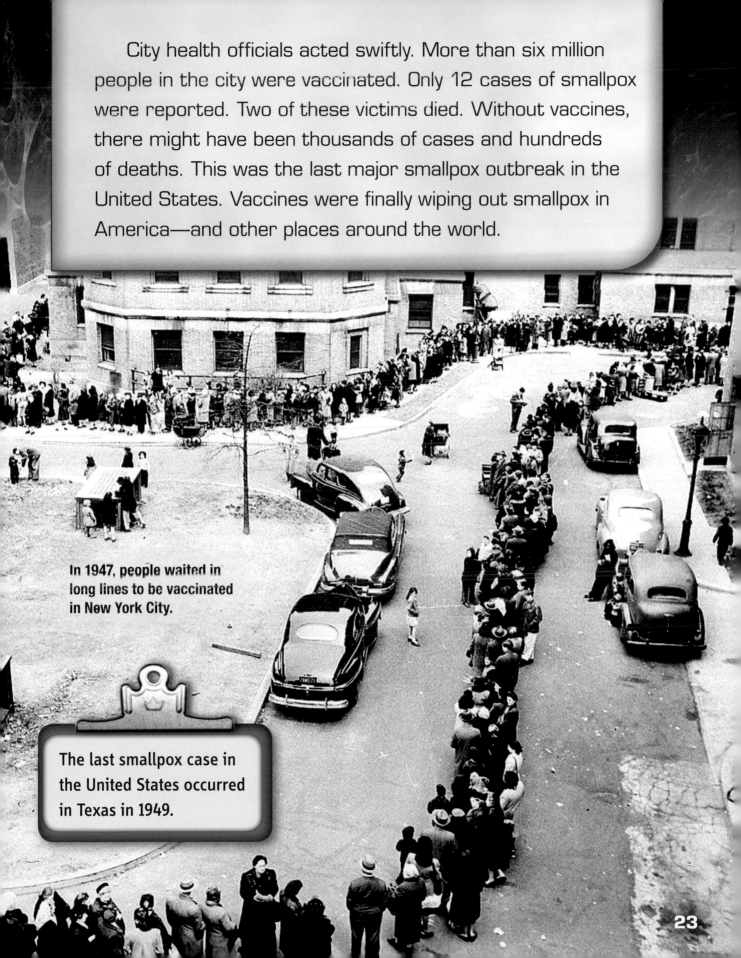

City health officials acted swiftly. More than six million people in the city were vaccinated. Only 12 cases of smallpox were reported. Two of these victims died. Without vaccines, there might have been thousands of cases and hundreds of deaths. This was the last major smallpox outbreak in the United States. Vaccines were finally wiping out smallpox in America—and other places around the world.

In 1947, people waited in long lines to be vaccinated in New York City.

The last smallpox case in the United States occurred in Texas in 1949.

The Last Victim?

Starting in the late 1960s, Dr. Frank Fenner worked as one of the leaders of the WHO project to destroy smallpox around the world. By 1977, it seemed as though their vaccination program had helped them reach their goal. Dr. Fenner hoped that Ali Maow Maalin would be the last person to ever have smallpox. To make sure, he waited about two years after Maalin got better. If, after that time, no new victims were reported, he would share some important news with the world. On May 8, 1980, he was ready.

People in West Africa waited in line for smallpox vaccinations during the WHO's program to wipe out the disease.

Fenner said, "The world and all its peoples have won freedom from smallpox, which was a most **devastating** disease . . . leaving death, blindness, and disfigurement in its wake." Finally, the world's greatest killer was defeated— or was it?

WORLD HEALTH

THE MAGAZINE OF THE WORLD HEALTH ORGANIZATION · MAY 1980

Smallpox is the only disease that has been wiped out by medicine.

smallpox is dead !

Scientists have estimated that so far about 60 million lives have been saved from smallpox because of the efforts of Dr. Fenner and his colleagues.

Will Smallpox Return?

Today, the only known smallpox viruses left in the world are locked up in two laboratories—one in the United States and one in Russia. Both countries agreed to store the viruses for research. Scientists can learn a lot about how to fight diseases by studying them.

Smallpox viruses are kept safely locked away in laboratories similar to this one in the United States.

However, some scientists today say the viruses should be destroyed. They fear that **terrorists** may already have gotten hold of some of the viruses, and will use them to kill people.

Other scientists believe this is unlikely. They point out that it is not easy to keep the smallpox virus alive. For example, the virus can be killed by high temperatures or direct sunlight. These scientists are convinced that one of the world's greatest killers will never strike again.

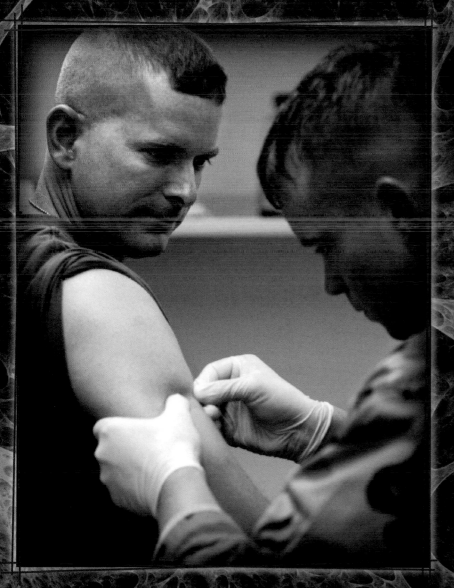

The U.S. government stopped giving smallpox vaccines to soldiers in 1990. Soon after the terrorist attacks of September 11, 2001, however, all American soldiers started getting the vaccine again.

The United States has taken steps to protect people from the possibility of terrorists spreading smallpox. The government has enough smallpox vaccine for everyone in the country.

Famous Smallpox Outbreaks

In the past, smallpox caused great suffering and killed hundreds of millions of people. Here are two outbreaks that were particularly deadly.

The Great Epidemic, 1775–1782

- The smallpox outbreak that attacked many of George Washington's soldiers during the American Revolution was part of a larger epidemic that struck all of North America.

- The disease hit both colonists and Native Americans very hard. Neither of these groups had strong immunity to smallpox like Europeans did.

- From 1775 to 1782, around 125,000 people in North America died from the epidemic.

India Epidemic, 1974

- In 1974 a deadly smallpox epidemic hit areas of eastern India. That year, the country had more than 80 percent of the world's smallpox cases.

- The epidemic occurred during the time of the WHO's program to destroy smallpox. Setbacks such as flooding prevented WHO workers from reaching some areas of India and vaccinating many people.

- About 25,000 people were reported to have been killed by this epidemic. It was one of the world's last major outbreaks of smallpox.

- In May 1975, a 30-year-old woman got the last reported smallpox case in India.

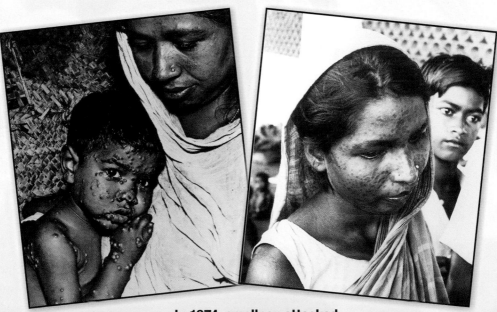

In 1974, smallpox attacked thousands of people in India, including this young boy and woman.

Smallpox Facts

Smallpox got its name from the word that people once used for pustules—pox. Here are some more facts about smallpox.

Famous People Who Had Smallpox

- Queen Elizabeth I (1533–1603), Queen of England—survived
- King Louis XV (1710–1774), King of France—died
- George Washington (1732–1799), President of the United States—survived
- Wolfgang Amadeus Mozart (1756–1791), composer—survived
- Andrew Jackson (1767–1845), President of the United States—survived
- Ludwig van Beethoven (1770–1827), composer—survived
- Abraham Lincoln (1809–1865), President of the United States—survived

President Abraham Lincoln had a mild case of smallpox when he served as President in the 1860s.

Smallpox Emergency Plan

The Centers for Disease Control and Prevention (CDC), a U.S. government agency, suggests the following action plan to limit the spread of smallpox if an outbreak should ever occur.

- Public health officials will use television, radio, newspapers, and the Internet to let people know how to protect themselves.
- Officials will tell people where to go for care if they think they have smallpox.
- Smallpox patients will be quarantined so healthy people around them do not get sick. The patients will get the best medical care possible.
- People who have had contact with a smallpox patient will be offered smallpox vaccinations as soon as possible to prevent infection. Then the people who have had contact with those individuals will also be vaccinated.
- The smallpox vaccine may also be offered to those who have not been exposed but would like to be vaccinated.

Glossary

cells (SELZ) the basic, microscopic parts of an animal or plant

conquerors (KONG-kur-*urz*) people who defeat others

devastating (DEV-uh-*stay*-ting) damaging, very upsetting

estimated (ESS-ti-*mayt*-id) to have figured out the approximate amount of something

exposed (ek-SPOHZD) made open to possible infection by a disease

fever (FEE-vur) a rise in one's body temperature to a point that is above normal—98.6°F (37°C)

immune (i-MYOON) protected from a disease

infected (in-FEK-tid) filled with harmful germs

infection (in-FEK-shuhn) an illness caused by germs entering the body

invades (in-VAYDZ) enters by force or takes over, usually in a harmful way

organs (OR-guhnz) parts of the body, such as the lungs or the heart, that do particular jobs

outbreak (OUT-*brayk*) a sudden spread of a disease among a group of people

plague (PLAYG) a disease that spreads quickly and often kills many people

protein (PROH-teen) a kind of substance that keeps the body healthy and strong

pus (PUHSS) the liquid that comes out of an infected wound or sore

pustules (PUHSS-choolz) growths on the skin similar to pimples filled with pus

quarantined (KWOR-uhn-*teend*) separated from others and not allowed to move around in order to prevent the spread of a disease

rash (RASH) red spots that occur on the skin, often caused by an illness

smallpox (SMAWL-*poks*) a disease caused by a virus that spreads among people and causes symptoms such as high fever and pustules that can leave permanent scars; it is often deadly

symptoms (SIMP-tuhmz) signs of a disease or other physical problems felt by a person

terrorists (TER-ur-ists) individuals or groups that use violence and terror to get what they want

theory (THEER-ee) an idea or belief based on limited information

vaccinated (VAK-suh-*nay*-tid) gave medicine, usually in shot form, that helps protect against disease

variolation (*vair*-ee-uh-LAY-shuhn) the introduction of smallpox into people's bodies so that they become protected from the disease in the future

virus (VYE-ruhss) a tiny germ that can be seen only with a powerful microscope; it can invade cells and cause disease

World Health Organization (WURLD HELTH *or*-guh-nuh-ZAY-shuhn) a United Nations agency made up of doctors, scientists, and other health workers that monitors disease outbreaks and works to improve the health of people around the globe; also known as the WHO

Bibliography

Crosby, Alfred W., Jr. *The Columbian Exchange: Biological and Cultural Consequences of 1492.* Westport, CT: Praeger Publishers (2003).

Henderson, Donald A. *Smallpox: The Death of a Disease.* Amherst, NY: Prometheus Books (2009).

video.nationalgeographic.com/video/player/science/health-human-body-sci/health/smallpox-sci.html

www.pbs.org/gunsgermssteel/variables/smallpox.html

Read More

Brown, Alan. *The Smallpox Slayer: One Man's Fight Against a Deadly Disease.* London: Hodder Children's Books (2001).

Giblin, James Cross. *When Plague Strikes: The Black Death, Smallpox, AIDS.* New York: HarperCollins (1997).

Marrin, Albert. *Dr. Jenner and the Speckled Monster: The Search for the Smallpox Vaccine.* New York: Dutton Children's Books (2002).

Ridgway, Tom. *Smallpox (Epidemics: Deadly Diseases Throughout History).* New York: Rosen (2001).

Learn More Online

To learn more about smallpox, visit
www.bearportpublishing.com/NightmarePlagues

Index

About the Author

Adam Reingold lives in New York City. On most
days he can look across the East River and see the
Roosevelt Island Smallpox Hospital, built in 1854
and abandoned in the 1950s.